Win before the fight

A journey into understanding

PAUL IUDICA

Foreword

I would like to begin with gratitude. I am so very thankful for all the positive influences in my life and the authors of the many books that I have read to deepen my awareness of truth and love. Names such as Napoleon Hill, Kyle Cease, Scott Alexander, Tony Robbins, Sri Mooji, Eckhart Tolle, Esther and Jerry Hicks, Wayne Dyer, Ralph Waldo Emerson and Joseph Murphy. There are too many to list but these have had the most profound impact on me. I am very thankful for having a mother who raised me with love and patience. I can literally attribute my entire existence and success to her. Whether she was picking me up from jail or taking me to my soccer game, she has always been there for me, and she always will be. All of my experiences and hardships in life have combined to bring me to the awareness that I am currently at. It's a wonderful time to be alive! Through my darkest days I was able to somehow manage to continue getting better. I always had something inside me tell me that there was more than I was experiencing. And I think this is true for everyone. There is always much more than you currently are, more to learn and a much greater person for you to develop into. That is the beautiful thing about being human, we literally have unlimited potential to unlock at any given moment. I hope you discover this wonderful truth and start living the life you want to live.

Chapter 1

It begins

The idea of writing a book is really nerve racking to me. Patience has never been a virtue of mine and I understand that a book cannot be possibly written entirely within one hour, so the commitment to finish once I start makes me a little anxious. I have never been someone who takes a long time to do something. I love things like lightning, crotch rockets, and fireworks. I am the poster child for instant gratification, and I think there are many other human beings that can understand this and perceive my struggle here. Writing a book… Well, I can say my biggest reason for actually doing this is the tremendous impact that other books have had on my own life, and somehow I wish to also positively impact others in this special way. I understand it's a long shot to say that you will identify with all of the things I mention in this book, but hopefully one or two things really stand out and help you advance in your personal journey through life.

Actually sitting down to do this is initially a pretty cool feeling. Now I can tell people I'm writing a book even if I have only just started. The beginning is part of every process right? I have always been a people pleaser so somewhere deep down I still feel a bit of acceptance when other people tell me encouraging things or show excitement because of my accomplishments. And honestly there is nothing wrong with that, as long as the feeling you get is not your number one reason for finding meaning and acceptance in yourself. Your unshakeable and true identity will come from within you, and although you may be a people pleaser like me, you will one day understand that true happiness can only be found within, if you have not already developed this understanding.

So, seeing as this is the first chapter, I feel like I want to make an introduction of myself. My name is Paul Alexander Iudica, I'm 33 years old. I was born on May 27th, 1984. Yes, I'm a Gemini. And I might remind you of that a few times throughout this book, because that's what we do. I'm sure that your sign is cool too, but not like mine. Kidding… Sarcasm has never been my stronghold either so I can only halfway pretend. But, I did read one time that people who are good at sarcasm seem to be more intelligent than those who don't use sarcasm often. So maybe I just lack intelligence.

I grew up on Long Island and moved to Texas around 8 years old. I've played soccer my whole life and once tried out for the Houston Dynamo Professional MLS team. I did not make it, obviously. I lived a very rebellious life from childhood to age 25. Dad passed when I was 3 years old from lung cancer

and mom did her best job to raise me, but I was a bit spoiled and lacked that disciplinary male figure in the early development years. I found drugs and alcohol at age 16 and that was my meal ticket for the next 8-10 years. Because you see, I had no identity growing up. My role model was Jean Claude Van Damme, and I had no idea what it was like to develop into my own self. So when I put drugs or alcohol into my body, it gave me this false sense of confidence that allowed me to feel good about myself, for once.
Unfortunately so many kids get caught up in stuff like this, and it's even much worse today in our society. Anyway, fast forward some time and I finally cleaned my life up and began a journey of self-improvement, and like I said before, it's my hope that this book can guide you back to yourself and find meaning like you have never known before.

    I'd like to basically just share with you some of the things I have learned throughout my journey. We all are given special gifts when we are born into this life. Some of my gifts include empathy, discernment, intuition, and understanding. Of course it took me some time to come into my own personal journey and my strengths, and to even realize that I had any. Just like many of you have not truly realized yours yet. The journey towards developing your most authentic self will take a curiosity and a desire to learn. Surprisingly many people do not even have this desire, or they have not seen enough struggles in life to search for answers to the pain in their hearts. I do believe in life the people who have seen the darkest days tend to be the spiritual gurus with the greatest understanding. Because the fact that you are reading this book tells me that you do have a desire to understand and learn more about yourself, so good for you!

      I'd love to know more about you and your personal journey. I really enjoy one on one connection with people. I have never really enjoyed being in crowds or surface conversations about stuff that doesn't really matter. Maybe somehow I can develop a way to connect to my readers, but I don't have any idea yet. I'd like to maybe sit down with randomly chosen people and talk to them about their experience with this book. That would be cool. Yes, I think I will do that. Ok great, now how about we move on to chapter 2 and get this show on the road.

Chapter 2

New

Ok, I know this is the beginning of chapter two but I have no idea where I even want to start. I am certainly putting too much thought into this and I need to just relax and think about my awesome cat Leo, or eating collard greens from a can, or screaming out the window of a moving vehicle and scaring cows grazing in a beautiful green pasture. Ok there we go, now I feel a little bit lighter. There is so much to touch on so I think the best thing would be for me to pick a title for chapter two? What rhymes with two? .... New! New certainly rhymes with two! "New" will be the title of chapter two. Great, that was easy enough. I'm going to continue rhyming my way through each chapter until this book is complete. What an awesome inspiring idea universe, thank you.

What is the first thing you think about when you hear the word new? Is it a shiny new Lamborghini, or maybe a nice new pair of Nikes? When we think of the word new, since this book is really going to be geared at self-improvement and personal growth, let's think of a new mindset or a new beginning. Even religious books and many teachings have much to say about new beginnings, and being reborn. The fact is that as each individual human being develops through life there will no doubt be new beginnings that one will undergo, which causes a massive transformation of mind and spirit through a renewal of ones beliefs. This should not be a shock to you, but I know also that some people are not aware that they have the ability to actually change themselves, or their mindset, and that is something that is very sad. You see it every day when you interact with people. Maybe even right now in your life you know someone who is stuck in a mindset that is no longer serving them, and they might feel that they are hopeless and doomed to live that way forever. This actually is very evident in unhappy people. They are in a deep and dark place that they feel they cannot climb out of. Maybe you are the one that will inspire someone out of their darkness.

    It's a shame that some of us settle in life. People settle for less than their best, or they just don't believe in themselves enough to feel worthy of anything better. This can be a cumulative result of a rough childhood, or any emotional trauma that might have been experienced in life. But honestly, we all have the ability to change, no matter what. I always say it's never too late to be the best version of yourself you can be, and it's true! You can literally start right now. I highly encourage it.

    So what does it mean to you to be the best version of yourself? To me it means that you have taken the time and effort to learn about your true self. The things you love in life. What makes you tick? What your absolute favorite things about yourself are and even the things you don't like about yourself. Being the best version of yourself means accepting yourself and loving yourself completely. This means all the good and all the bad. Working through your depression, sadness, and anger that you have once experienced and coming out on the other side of these emotions stronger than you were before. It means being proud of yourself and finding value within your soul. Knowing that there is not another human being on this planet exactly like you, and that you have the right to be anything you want to be, and do anything you want to do, providing there are no harmful consequences of course. If you wanted to blow bubbles and walk down the sidewalk singing songs, that'd be fine, but I don't think it would be a good idea to run naked across a busy freeway shouting obscenities. At that point other human beings would have to step in and control you.

So how does someone become the best version of themselves? What kind of time and effort does this take? Well, I guess it all depends on where you start. The easiest way I could answer this would be with one word, education. But surely not the education that comes to your mind when you hear that word. I am not talking about the school system, college or anything that is common in our society.

The kind of education I am describing here is of a higher value. There is a certain calling within you that desires to find understanding. There are certain voids in your heart that can only be filled with certain levels of acceptance of what is. What is true? What is real? So, the most important thing to become the best version of yourself is by being subjected to the truth, and learning more about the reality of your existence. By understanding that you can escape the grasp of the societal norms, and begin to realize that our entire system on this planet is not the most beneficial for the whole human race, you can begin to feel the unity that lives within your heart, and realize there is no division amongst all living things.

Being exposed to truth and wisdom does a few things to your mindset. One of the first things you realize when you begin to understand and seek the truth is that it will excite you tremendously! You will have this overwhelming desire to understand things deeply, and to know all the details about situations and events you find in your life. But, on the other hand the truth can also hurt you. I always believe that being hurt by the truth is a bittersweet but beautiful thing. In the beginning there is pain but after the pain there is freedom. And this freedom can only be attained by establishing a relationship with the truth.

Many people will find the truth through religion, and this can be very rewarding and encourage personal growth within the soul of someone. There is a certain acceptance that people will feel when they are around other people who believe the same thing as they do. But if someone desires a deeper wisdom and understanding, I believe you have to get outside the walls of any one certain religious belief. As you progress in life you cannot remain as the same person you were when you were 5 years old, and this goes with your belief system also. Your understanding of God or source energy, the universe or whatever you call it should constantly be evolving, because your awareness never stops developing and every day you are becoming a better version of yourself than the previous day. Of course this is not the case with everyone. Many people in life are stagnant, or comfortable. These people almost refuse to develop themselves any further for whatever reason. A person's religion surely plays a role in this also, because even for Christians and Muslims alike, many of them believe that they should never question anything that they find in their religious book, or set out on their own personal journey to grow closer to God. They use their religious text as the one and only tool that they have to educate themselves about life. The journey toward the truth never stops, so if one really wants to seek it they must have a desire to step outside of their comfort zone, societal norm, or more importantly their own religion.

Now don't get me wrong I'm not knocking religion by any means. All I am saying is religion can only take you so far, and I truly believe this in my heart. The rest of the journey towards God, or the universe, or existence completely depends on you. The amount of effort you put into learning more about humanity, consciousness, and our history will directly affect the level of awareness you attain in life. The more you seek, the more you will reveal, and the truth will come rushing towards you once you begin this amazing journey of self-discovery.

Speaking of self-discovery, let's shed some light on a very interesting topic. If you take a look at the bible, think about the very first thing that is mentioned in the idea of creation. It is light. Light is the very first thing that "started" our existence. Light comes from the sun, if I'm not mistaken. Now if you are on this new journey of diving into a deeper understanding of the truth let's look at the similarity of this idea. Ancient Egyptians, being one of the oldest people on earth, had a very deep respect and understanding of the sun. They saw the sun as this great life bringer, and rightly so. Without the sun there would be no life on earth, and without life on earth we would not be here. So, you see how if you open the bible for instance and read "God said let there be light", and then we look at the reverence also that the Egyptians had for the sun, which is where the light comes from, you can begin to feel the connection that human beings have to the light, right? Ancient Egypt was around long before the bible was even written, and these people were already connected to this great understanding of the sun, and light. This kind of stuff excites me!

So, in my opinion it's safe to say that the sun and light are two very important factors to life on earth, do you agree? Great!

So if life comes from light, then we should seek to learn more about light if we want to understand more of who we are as human beings. You may have heard the term "light beings". In the religion of Buddhism, when one attains a certain level of peace and understanding that surpasses a normal mindset that person is said to become enlightened. There is no coincidence here. This beautiful word simply means that the person's mindset, or consciousness, has returned to the light. The divine connection within that represents connection and unity with source, which is light, or God. Are you getting goosebumps yet or is it just me?

So being that the chapter title is new I feel I need to stay focused on this before I start talking about energy too much. We will save that for later. If you seek to change anything about your mindset or your beliefs then you must become new, and set aside old beliefs that no longer serve you. Like I said before, this journey in life is a journey of constant growth. If you are not seeking growth in body, mind, and spirit daily then you might as well be dead. And many people are dead, on the inside. It's funny how we talk about the Zombie apocalypse and there are countless movies and shows about this concept, when all the while this is actually already happening. People already are the walking dead. When you look into the eyes of someone you can actually feel their soul, if you slow down enough and tune into it. I can literally walk in the mall and point out "Zombies", or people who are dead inside. These people are the ones who have given up on life, or who have settled for a life that is less than their best. They are just existing and not thriving. They are drifting, and not really aware that they have the potential to be or do anything they want in life, and the only one that controls this is them.

    Part of my reason for being on this planet is to wake people up, and this book is a step in that journey, and I'm excited to see where my calling takes me. I hope that after reading this book you have a better understanding of life and your own personal journey, and your special calling. I'm asking you to join me on this epic transition into authenticity and awareness. To maybe actually meet yourself for the very first time. To throw off the old ideas of society that you have grown up with, and start living the life you want to live, because you can. And you're supposed to!

Chapter 3

Free

Three rhymes with free so yep you guessed it, free is the title of chapter three. This is by far the coolest way to think of chapter names. And I thought this was going to be the hard part, hah! Naming chapters is a piece of cake.

So let's pick back up where we left off from chapter new. I was speaking about your journey into authenticity. It is actually so appropriate that this chapter is named free, because living an authentic life and being in tune with yourself will cause your heart to feel so free that you literally float through each day like a balloon. Trust me.

If your freedom is a hot air balloon, then your authenticity is the fuel that keeps the fire burning. One thing we really get hung up on in life is attachments. People will actually depend on their attachment to things to provide their happiness. Maybe it's that fancy new car in their driveway that makes them smile every day and wake up excited to go to work. Or maybe it's an attachment to a significant other that produces joy and excitement. Whatever the attachment, the happiness that is felt from any material thing outside of yourself is only temporary happiness. Now don't get me wrong material things and temporary happiness are absolutely amazing. In fact I love that feeling of having something new, I think we all do! But there is a time when that excitement will wear off and you will be thrown back into a sort of depression until you have another sequence of temporary happiness come into your life from something that is outside of you. What I mean by something outside of you is that anything that makes you happy in the physical or material world will not be the most authentic happiness that you can attain. And if we are being honest with ourselves and really wanting to seek the best life possible, and develop into our most authentic selves, then we must be willing to understand that real fulfillment and true happiness must come from within you.

What in the hell does that even mean? Is this some hippie shit? What do you mean within? How do I get there? These questions are making me laugh because in my mind I'm doing them in a redneck accent and it's absolutely phenomenal. You're welcome.

So here is where the freedom part comes in. We are the only ones that can determine our happiness in life, and that is true freedom. You are in complete control of your emotions one hundred percent of the time. So knowing that you can control your happiness and that it's found within you is like a great transcending staircase that goes up to the heavens, and ignites the divine connection that you have to the radiant light, or God. This is your true nature. Your connection to this being, or this never ending energy, is the source of the greatest happiness you will ever know. Now I'm not saying that people who don't have a connection to something greater than themselves cannot be happy, but I'm willing to bet they don't feel the same fulfillment in life, or have peace of mind. And again this has nothing to do with religion, or it might have everything to do with religion, depending on your personal belief system.

     Ok we know that we need a connection to something within us, and that connection and deep understanding can provide something that nothing outside of us will ever compare to. Let's move on. This source energy, God or Great Spirit is found within the life of every living thing, but let's look at how we all have the power to choose what we believe and how that affects our happiness, and our freedom. As you grow up you are introduced to many ideas of God. You can be raised Catholic like I was, or be raised to believe that humans are just a physical body and that's that. And this is where the human experience gets absolutely wonderful. The fact above all else is that nobody knows all the answers. Religions are a group of people's best effort to identify this life, and this Great Spirit, or their best effort to find meaning and connection with something greater than themselves, and then they create a whole teaching based around it. That's all religion is really. It is just a man's explanation of the source that connects all living things, and his/her experiences within that energy. When people so frequently say God told me this, or God told me that, they are really just tapping into a place of completeness, and when you are in that place any answer to any question you will ever imagine can be answered. Now, you can see why happiness truly comes from within because the greatest source of unhappiness is ignorance, or this feeling of lack, or not having enough. But when you tap into your divine energy you never ever have to have a feeling of lack because your guidance and direction will come directly from the storehouse of infinite intelligence, and all your answers can be found within you. Let's use the word love because this word represents God also. When you are connected to love, you have everything you need within you. When you are not connected to love, you will constantly seek material things or experiences or relationships to give you small pieces of love, but not the wholeness that you are truly seeking.

     I could start my own religion if I wanted to, but I try not to even really use that word too much. And it's funny because I actually was very religious at one time in my life, a Christian. I went to church on Sundays and could quote the bible, and thought that if people didn't believe in Jesus then they were going to hell. What a very interesting time in my life that was, but I honestly would not be here today if It was not for my relationship with Jesus. I have many relationships that have influenced my spiritual journey. There is not only one way to find that divine connection to you and whatever you believe in. There just isn't. If you find this offensive, that's perfectly ok. Everyone has their own level of consciousness and understanding, and I completely respect that. There are many rivers but they all reach the sea. All religions and spiritual teachings point in a similar direction. To say that there is only one way is something I don't agree with.

So authenticity not only allows you to be free and live a more fulfilled life, but it also naturally invites other people to do the same. Energy is contagious, and when you are living from the most authentic part of your heart people feel that, and it gives them courage to not only step into a more true version of themselves, but to also be a beacon of light for the next person. And so the saga continues. This amazing balance of life and love and understanding is beautiful, and as many people as there are on this planet, are as many ways to find and understand life and love, and a connection to your divinity.

You have such a huge impact on people that it's almost unbelievable. Your individual life can literally influence and encourage millions of others. Something about that just amazes me and gives me so much hope while writing this book. Some of the greatest people that walked this earth came here to teach service and love. In fact, I think service to others is one of the most profound teachings. Allowing yourself to connect to this energy of love and care about another person can completely transform not only you, but the person you are compassionate for also. You're most authentic self can also be found while showing this love and kindness to others, because when you are tapped into this energy of love you are actually being powered by the source energy, or God. So this means that learning what you have to offer others and encouraging them in their journey is also a way for you to develop your own personal relationship with the Great Spirit of life. The two go hand in hand.

    People say God is found in nature and I completely agree. There is no greater concentration of source energy than when you are amongst the trees or standing on the side of a mountain. You somehow feel so deeply connected to something that it makes your stomach tight with anxiety. But it's not a bad anxiety, it's a good anxiety. The kind of anxiety that gives you butterflies. The kind of feeling that you get when you smell your grandmas cooking or take the first sip of sweet iced tea on a hot summer day. There is just something deep inside you that feels good. That feeling is the feeling that we should live in, every second of every day.

Actually feeling good is something that is super important and I'd love to explain. Think of yourself like a magnet. And your heart and your brain are like tools you use to attract stuff to you. You attract with your mind by the thoughts you think and you attract with your heart by the emotions that you feel. This is something that is constantly happening 24/7. You cannot press stop or pause. This amazing sequence of energy exchange is an actual law that governs our universe. It's called the law of attraction, and I'm sure you have heard of it by now. So yea you might have heard about this law or watched YouTube videos about it but maybe you do not understand the most important part of this law. The brain and the heart both emit a frequency. The Institute of Heart Math conducted an experiment and found that the electronic signal that the heart emits is 60 times stronger than the one the brain emits. For the longest time I thought the mind was the main power in our life, but realistically and magnetically the heart is a much more powerful tool than the mind.

Ok so you understand what this means about feeling good right? If your heart is 60 times more powerful than your mind than not only is it important to feel more than you think, but this is the way that you can invite the universe to work on your behalf and start to give you all that you desire in life. Remember your heart is emitting an electrical frequency and we live in an electromagnetic universe.

These two things are facts. When you are in a place of freedom and feeling good you are emitting that energy out into the universe, and the universe has to respond magnetically and send back the exact energy that you are giving off. Because like attracts like, remember you're a magnet. So bottom line is to feel good and stay in the place of freedom as much as possible, because by doing so you will attract everything that you need and want into your life, and you will start to realize how beautiful and effortless this existence can be.

In this effortlessness is freedom.

Chapter 4

More

The title to chapter 4 is more. This is possibly going to be one of the best chapters because this is a disease that infects the society of our culture and can cause the greatest pain and suffering in life. Suffering is also a choice but we can talk about that later. I don't think there is a number that rhymes with suffering so it probably can't be the title to a chapter, so maybe I'll just magically tie it in here with this chapter.

Ok so why would I say more is a disease? Well because in life people are never satisfied and once they obtain something it quickly becomes not enough and then they must have the next best thing or the next version or whatever. People are not happy with themselves so they are always looking for more and more and more. This goes back to the idea that happiness is found within, remember. If you have real authentic happiness then you are immune to the disease of more, and you obtain things specifically for personal preference and not for fulfilment to something deeper.

I honestly do not think American society would flourish if not for the disease of more. In fact our economy would probably collapse. Wow I literally just had an epiphany about this. Our economy and those in control do not want people to be genuinely happy because that would cut down on the necessity to seek fulfilment in material things, and therefore the media and the corporations constantly prime the minds of those who watch giving them this illusion that if they buy this product they will be happy. Crazy isn't it? I guess when you see the bigger picture you can begin to understand how much is wrong. Despite living in this society and culture there is also so much to be grateful for and the fact of the matter is this. People are starting to wake up to the reality that is, and raising their awareness to truth and wisdom. This is really a great time to be alive!

So why do people continue to seek more, even if they already have enough? Why are we not ever satisfied? The most clear and direct answer is because people are in constant search outside of themselves to make the inside feel good. This is a clear picture of what I have already spoken about in the aspect where true happiness and authenticity comes from within, and until someone can learn to be authentically happy from the inside they will always want more. Having more is not always a bad thing, but in a sense of greediness or gluttony it's certainly horrible. Suffering comes into play when the subject is in a state of wanting and therefore undergoes an intense agitation of the mind until what they want is attained, and then in due time the process starts over with something else. This constant state of wanting is something very common in the Western culture. In Buddhism they teach you how to be in a state of peace through meditation, not wanting anything. Of course using this example is pretty extreme because it's hard enough to get the common American to slow down enough to clear their mind, let alone actually meditate and reach a state of peace, if only for a short time.

It seems the key to most of our problems can be found when we slow down and turn within our hearts and minds. This is so true on so many levels and that's why this idea of being authentic and honest with yourself centers on connecting with this divine source inside of you. I'm afraid without this connection one cannot really experience the magnetic power of the law of attraction by using the energy and frequency of a happy heart to pull all your desires and dreams towards you. So many people are conditioned to believe they have to work hard for money and hustle harder to achieve the things they want, and I just don't believe it's true. If you really want to achieve the things you want in life then learn more about yourself, and in turn God will reveal the many secrets of the universe to you, and you will realize that you are part of this vast expanse of light and love, ever developing your consciousness to drift in the flow of the natural world, without fight or struggle.

Of course people will hear this idea and claim that it is absolutely crazy. That if you want something you have to work hard for it. And nothing good comes easy. Well, that is just what they have been conditioned their whole lives to believe. Can you begin to understand how these things work? You see, many ideas and thoughts have been passed down for years and years and we are at a beautiful time in history to be learning all the stuff that we are and we are breaking through our old mindsets and discovering something wonderful and true about the universe and the direct effect that our mind and hearts have on it. Think of science as the most accurate way to engage in the process of learning how to have anything and be anything in life. WE are so balanced within certain equations of time and space that we can send a man to the moon! The human race now understands how the heart and the mind are intertwined within this great cosmic energy and this gives us the ability to be masters of our own lives, creators of the identity and existence that we want for ourselves.

So let's get back to this crisis of people never being satisfied and always wanting more. I believe in order for someone to attain a higher awareness or enlightened state of being one has to be subject to enough pain and suffering to even begin to look for answers. I am afraid that people who have everything handed to them in life and never have to struggle simply cannot get to a point where they are so sick and tired that they begin their own journey back to self, spirit, and light. But these are the people that flourish our society and isn't that what we want as a whole? We want people to chase after material things and stimulate the economy so that the greedy can feed their disease, and the factory worker can make a paycheck and go home and feed their family.

Now I cannot claim to understand everything about the soul or the spirit but I can speak from experience and personal intuition. If I hadn't gone through so much pain and suffering in life then clearly I would have not decided to accept Jesus and begin my spiritual journey. Because at the time I was hurting and I could not see any other way, so it was a last resort to maybe give this whole religious church thing a try, so I did, and I'm thankful for my willingness. If it was not for a good friend named Brittany, who knows if I would have showed up at that church that day. The church was a nondenominational Christian church. But it was only because of my pain and suffering I was experiencing that I decided to turn to something bigger than myself, something we call God. Like I said this was only the beginning of my journey and understanding. I was 18 and I needed direction and hope. I'm very grateful for Christianity and the bible, but it was only the start of what would become the most amazing journey I think one human being can partake in.

So having discussed what it is to constantly be seeking more and looking for answers in the physical life rather than diving into the spirit and mind, I wanted to speak about the internal guidance that is found when you begin to take the journey within. I would like you to think of this as your intuition, or your gut feeling. We are all familiar with this feeling. The tightness in your stomach when you know you shouldn't be doing something or the feeling of bliss and joy when you act from your heart and make someone smile. This internal guidance system might be the most amazing tool you have in this life. The reason I say that is because this guidance system is directly connected with God, or the universe. This Great Spirit of life resides inside of you at all times and all you have to do is slow down enough to feel it and tap into it. But in our society, like I was saying, people are so focused on what is outside of them that they never even consider anything inside of them. Some people don't even know what the word intuition means. So clearly the problem is ignorance correct? Because if more people knew more about the power that is within them there would be more books written, more seminars conducted, and more lives changed for the better. The fact of the matter is that once you become enlightened to the power that you have inside of you then you no longer have to look for more in a physical sense, in a material world. The whole world becomes a library of wisdom to learn more about this Great Spirit we call God and the connection that you have within to attract and become anything you want in life.

Living in a state of always wanting more comes from a duality belief. This is a belief that I am always in competition with someone else and that I must out do the next guy rather than understanding that everything is connected in life and whatever someone else has, you have it also. There is no separation. There is no I am better or he is better. WE are all so connected that it is impossible for you completely fathom, but since the downfall of consciousness we have come to believe that we are all separated by race, religion and identity. I cannot say what the future will hold for our planet but some of us are called in this life to defend humanity and to bring unity once again to a fallen kingdom. To encourage enlightenment in others and to cause people to look for answers, or to question their faith instead of following blindly toward something that they do only to fit in. I'm here to motivate you to find your own truth, and in turn help others do the same. And to know there is no separation between us. There is no separation of God. There is no separation of love. Not by religion, race or identity. We are all ONE.

This is SO much bigger than anything we have ever known. So many living beings have died because of ideas and beliefs. This is such a great time to be alive because so many people are waking up. We are beginning to find ourselves again as humanity and we are moving back towards a collective consciousness that will one day unite all human beings and life on earth.

So I invite you to become part of this special internal guidance system that you have. Do not continue looking outside of you for the next best thing. Do not constantly look for more and more. You have everything you will ever need, and once you can understand that and feel it you'll be transformed into something amazing and I'm almost sure that you will set out on your own personal journey to define and understand this vast expanse that is our universe, and God. Do this, and encourage others to do the same. Join arms and let's make this planet beautiful. There is a great love that is found in spending time helping and serving others. Remember after all service to others is the greatest teaching that has ever been discovered.

Let's move on.

Chapter 5

No rhyme or reason

Ok now that I have begun this whole flow of writing and picking chapter titles by rhyming I'm going to stop. The fantastical way of choosing chapter titles was fun while it lasted, but it's time to be more serious. Although 5 does rhyme with thrive, and I could really expand on thriving, I just don't want to pick chapter names like this anymore. I'm just being honest with myself and following that inner guidance. Can you imagine if I make it to chapter sixteen? Seriously, what in the world would I do? How would I title a chapter "Thick Spleen", or "Fixed Bean"? It would be a nightmare, so game over for that insane brilliance.

In this life we are here to serve others. If your heart is filled with love and your mind is free then you will actually want to serve others, and bring value to the picture of our planet as a whole. You will begin to see how your individual experiences can benefit other people, and maybe you will write a book, or become a motivational speaker or perhaps you will get involved in a charity organization or volunteer your time to those in need. Donating money is a huge way to give in order to help others. Maybe become a coach and teach kids the fundamentals of life, or how to be a successful human. There are numerous talents and gifts that you have to serve others and once you find what suits you it will no doubt transform your life into something beautiful and something much better than you could have ever imagined.

But too many people are chasing. The most common thing to chase is money, of course. We all want financial freedom and the ability to travel and do things we love. This is a great freedom to strive for but I'm here to tell you that there is a common misconception around making money. If you have read any books by Napoleon Hill, your eyes would no doubt be opened up to this great energy of money and the power we have to attain it in great quantities. The misconception has to do with societal norms once again as previously discussed. We have been so conditioned as a society to think that money takes hard work and long laboring hours and a career doing something that we don't really love, when it reality it's just not true. To be completely blunt money is an exchange of energy, like my buddy Mitch Newman once said. It is an exchange of whatever you believe it to be. If you believe you have to go work 50 hours a week as a store manager at a mattress store for the rest of your life, then you will be given that energy in exchange, and the money you will acquire will be a direct reflection of the thoughts you hold inside your mind about your job and about your future. But if you believe that anything is possible and that one day you will be swimming in money, then you will create that for yourself. Because of choosing to understand that if you are in a state of belief about anything, your belief has the absolute power to create that reality for you. And more so if you feel deeply the emotions of what it will feel like, you will cause the forces of the universe to partner with you on your journey towards your desires. The entire energy field that surrounds you is working for you. Whatever energy and emotion you are sending out is pulling the exact same back to you. So if you believe that one day you will have more than enough money, than you certainly will. But this doesn't mean you can sit on your ass and just have money handed to you. No, you have to stay in a place of sincerity and authenticity and gratitude. Move from your heart and stay in the energy of love and service to others. This is a sure way to guarantee everything you want in life, especially money.

      Your belief makes everything real, and I'm going to make a very bold statement and say that even God is not real without your belief in him/her. This should not shock you at all. Some of this scares people but it's only because they are still living in fear, but this is a great truth and reality of our existence. Your life will be completely based on what you believe. So you actually have a personal responsibility to develop your own belief system. It's not society or the church's job to tell you what to believe in, you have this individual right. And I think it's a wonderful thing that we get to experience! You have free will. You have the freedom to choose. You don't have to listen to anybody. You don't have to believe in other people's beliefs. It is my understanding that if you have a desire and an open mind then you will eventually come to a place of belief in something greater than you. Whether you choose to call it God or not is irrelevant. I mainly use the word God for convenience because it's very easy for most people to understand. But my perception of God is not like anyone else's, and I believe that's how it's supposed to be.

Living in your authenticity is a powerful way to enhance your belief system. If you are being honest with yourself and you simply cannot say that there is a God, then that is your belief. And if it is coming from an authentic and honest place, then who can argue with you. I can only praise you for following your heart and encourage you to continue to do so. The rest is out of mine and your hands. The energy of the universe will take care of it.

I would happily sit down and have a discussion with an honest atheist rather than sit down with a strict religious person. At least the atheist will admit to not knowing things. The religious person will quote scripture directly from their spiritual book and claim that it is THE truth. You see, one person comes from a place of authenticity I believe, and one comes from somebody else's interpretation. Of course this has only been my experience and what I have seen happen, I know not all religious people are like this, but many times they take things word for word straight out of their book without question. That's why it is so important to think on your own. You should not ever let society or religion delegate you're thinking forever. Of course we all start somewhere, like I mentioned before, I was a Christian for a number of years before I started to think for myself and uncover my own truth about life and God, and it's funny, the bible verse that comes to my mind is "Lean not on your own understanding….", so I think it's quite remarkable that today I feel so connected to love and light that I'm not scared of verses like that anymore, and I actually feel free to grow deeper in my relationship with this Great Spirit we call God, without being confined by religion, and actually leaning on my own understanding and being at peace with that.

So what are we all looking for? Do you think people are living in fear, and whatever they can find to divert them from that fear will become their belief system? Or, do you think people are just trying to belong to something?

I know as human beings the things we want the most are love, connection and a feeling of belonging. So in a sense being part of group who all believes in the same thing is exactly what we were meant to do. It gives us exactly what we are looking for. I guess there are some of us crazies who know that there is more to life and we cannot simply be satisfied with one belief for very long. In the sense of the last chapter I guess you can say that I have the disease of more. Yes, I am guilty. I have the desire to learn more. To always seek to obtain more wisdom and understanding about life and humanity. So you see we are more connected than even I understand.

But surely I think fear is the great motivator. I think it is by far the number one reason people develop a higher belief in life. I think the thing that drives people to church and religion is the fear of death. I know for a while I had that fear early on, which was one of the reasons I jumped into Christianity. Only one of the reasons, mind you. But after accepting Christ when I was 18, I was so relieved that I could basically simply choose to believe in Jesus and then be spared from a place of fire and torment called "hell", one day when I died. That was easy! Well, that fear of death was quickly diminished and I believe my next fear came much later in life and it was the fear of not knowing the truth. I knew that the bible taught me so much but it just wasn't enough for me, because I knew there was more, and I wanted to know as much as I could. Is that not the reason we are here, to learn and learn and learn and never stop learning? So this still is my current fear in life, my fear of not knowing the truth. Of course it is not something that keeps me up at night or even really bothers me too much, but I am someone who desires and seeks the truth no matter what. This is my calling and this is why I am here, to find the truth and encourage others to find it also.

In a society that has gotten so used to lies I find it increasingly hard to find honest, authentic people. In fact people are almost taken back when you speak the truth. There are so many illusions about life and the way we think things are that when someone comes in and speaks from an honest authentic place, it has the ability to completely shatter that person's belief system, and I think that is a beautiful thing, yet extremely scary for the person living in denial or illusion.

I will always show love and compassion for people, but I will never feel guilty for offending someone's beliefs by speaking the truth. If someone gets offended it's because that person doesn't actually fully believe in their own beliefs. Their foundation is shaky and if they are offended by another person's truth then maybe they should reconsider their own. I think this an amazing opportunity for that person to stop living their lie and break free from the confines of cultural conditioning. Of course rarely do you find someone who thinks like this also. From my experience most of the time they will consider you weird or strange, and create distance between you and them quickly. I don't blame them. What If I stepped into a circle full of Buddhist monks and told them that they cannot reach enlightenment until they follow Wakan Tanka to the top of the Rocky Mountains and perform a battle ceremony under the moon. That would be outrageous. In the Lakota Indian tribe Wakan Tanka is known as The Great Spirit, or Great Mystery. This is something we can equate to God.

To each man go his own journey and this great existence on planet earth is full of billions of people, all with separate beliefs and ideas. But still with this division among us, there is also this great connection we all share as human beings. This life energy that connects us, and this chance we have been given to be alive here on this earth in this universe is really unique, and who knows what is next in the great expanse that our universe is experiencing.

Science has proven that there are multiple galaxies and universes out there. Who is to say that there is not life in those other places, or that we don't' go there when we move on to begin a completely different life, in different bodies on a different planet. Seriously people, use your imagination. There is no end to what there might be out there, or what may lie right around the corner for us. Don't be confined by society or religion and let that delegate everything that you do or believe forever.

Have you ever just walked through the forest by yourself, and listened to the birds chirping and felt the gentle breeze blow across your face. Yes, it's amazing. As I am guessing you have done this at least once in your life. Now in that moment when you are walking do you feel small or big? Well, depending on how far you are away from society or the city you should feel small. If you're on the edge of a mountainside in the Himalayas then you should feel really small. The point I want to make is that although you feel small in that very moment it's actually one of the most powerful feelings of connection that you have felt with nature or the universe too, right? They say there is just something about being in nature that brings you close to God. Close to creation and this life energy connection that you share with the trees and the life around you. Deep within you can almost feel a force, a force of nature if you will? This force of nature can be tied back into this inner guidance system that I spoke about earlier. You have a force of nature that guides you, and you can always tap into this force and wait for guidance and answers to situations in life. Your true authentic self knows this, but you have to quiet down the noise inside your mind in order to hear and feel it. Sometimes this inner guide is like a voice you hear. Sometimes it's your voice talking to yourself in your own mind. Sometimes it's just a feeling you feel. Like a 6th sense of sorts that you know within, your gut feeling.

So why would I bring this inner guidance up and compare it to walking alone in the forest? Well, because that's exactly what it's like! This metaphor I used was to give you a deeper understanding of this power that lives inside of you, regardless of what you believe there is something that connects you to the rest of life, and once you learn to start listening to and feeling the emotions that come from this connection, the sooner you can have everything in life you've ever wanted.

Chapter 6

We three things

I've taken a few days off from writing so forgive me if I repeat anything or don't completely pick up where I left off. I attended a New Warrior Training (Men's retreat) this weekend as part of the Mankind Project, and I am now getting back to my everyday life rhythm. There is something unique about this moment in that there will never be another one exactly like it. Just like you reading this sentence right now, in this present moment. This will never happen again. Take a moment and just breathe that in.

We are able to live life on earth because of science. This is an undeniable truth of existence. We have a mother and a father, and after being conceived we start out as a single cell in our mother's womb. The beginning of our life starts with one cell, and that cell is the shape of a circle. The sun, the moon, and all the planets are also in the shape of a circle. There is a natural and beautiful relevance here, and I want you to take a moment to see that connection that we share with this….. We start as one cell, and in order to grow that one cell has to duplicate, and turn into an exact copy of itself, creating two cells. You could also say the cell has to get to know itself before moving onto the next stage of growth and evolving. The cellular duplication continues and in due time the first organ to develop is the heart.

Take a moment again to understand this great lesson….. The first cell that started your existence is the shape of a circle and the first organ to develop is your heart. Listen to your inner guidance right now and understand the great power that the circle and the heart have. Give thanks to your inner guidance for allowing you to feel that.

The sacred meaning to life and existence is something that no man will ever fully understand, but at least we can see relevance in some great truths, and share this wisdom within our heart and minds to find answers and push forward in our journey. Going back to authenticity we can start to feel a deeper connection to ourselves and how powerful our heart is in this magnitude of energy. Remember earlier that our heart is 60 times more powerful than our minds, and that living from our heart is the most sincere and authentic way to attract the energy of our desires, and create the life we have always dreamed of. The way we feel and expressing those emotions is something that we should never let our mind get in the way of. Always tap into your heart and feel the emotions therein. In every situation you can always turn inside to your heart and listen to your body for guidance, knowing that by doing so you are living your full potential, and all you have to do is honor that space within you. This is a great connection that goes overlooked by a large portion of human beings. I am hoping that by writing this book I can influence at least a handful of people to live more meaningful lives. But, I am also releasing myself of any expectation at the same time, knowing that by writing this book I am growing as a person also, and learning more about myself and my inner guidance, so therefore I am acting to benefit myself but by doing so I have the opportunity to benefit others also. Just like the flight attendant instructs you to put your oxygen mask on first before helping others. This book is part of my oxygen mask, and it is not yet complete so I cannot assist you yet with yours.

There are three elements to every human being and we have understood this for many years. The meaningful discovery that we have a BODY, with a MIND, and a SPIRIT is a common truth that we all share.

I believe each person's journey consists of finding balance within all three of these. The true path to authenticity is not letting one outweigh the other, but acknowledging each aspect and dedicating time and effort into the development therein. A man's spirit and mind cannot be healthy if his body is not also. The mind cannot be the only developed aspect as the other two will suffer. You can understand the pattern here... We must connect to our innermost selves by the awareness of spending time with each part of us. Educate your mind by reading books and obtaining wisdom. Search for answers and question everything. Develop your body by physical training and always staying active, and be mindful of the food and drink you put into your body. And let your spirit be free by letting go of anything that makes you feel heavy in life or any past hurts that still weigh you down. Also, become more spiritual by connecting to whatever source of power that you believe in, and continue to develop that energy. Remember there is no wrong belief here. You are your master.

So the word that comes to my mind right now is connection. Connection to self, and the authenticity that is uncovered when your body, mind and spirit are balanced and healthy. As you go through life you can be so in tune with yourself that you can feel when one of these three things needs attention. The idea is to find your joy and happiness within you, and listen to your body when it tells you what it is feeling. If you can understand that your internal guidance system is the most accurate and powerful way to show you the path you are supposed to take then you can start to live deliberately, and become the true creator of your future.

I believe we were all meant to live this way. But when did we ever learn this kind of knowledge in school? The answer is never. The public school system does not teach this wisdom because it does not align with the conditioning that we have been in for the past two hundred years. Our society wants to create more workers and more slaves to keep this money system working. The system which says we must go to school and make money. This is our main focus is it not? Of course there is the idea of settling down and having kids and one day retiring from your career in which the only reason for pursuing was your motivation to make money. Do you think oil executives are really passionate about oil? Do you think these guys really find meaning by drilling holes into the earth and sucking stuff out? I mean of course I am not speaking for them, because maybe there is a small handful that can say yes they absolutely love doing that, but there is also a great majority of people that can identify with a greater calling in life and cannot find true peace in a job like this.

   This higher calling is something I believe every man and woman has. I honestly think our reason for being here is to tap into that system and find out exactly why we are here. But there is a veil in front of the eyes of all human beings that prevents people from ever finding this true calling, because of their desire for money and material things. This veil keeps us blinded to the material dimension and the belief that there is nothing outside of this. This veil says the body is the only thing that represents us as humans, and that all physical things attainable in life will be the only things to bring happiness and joy. This veil blinds us to the confinement of our bodies and prevents us from uncovering truth. That is why for a human to find truth they must personally seek it. We must dedicate some time or perhaps our whole life to this journey towards truth. Other people may inspire or guide us but this journey is personal and individual to every man or woman. I encourage you on your journey.

      Think of life on earth as it is in heaven. Just like in "Our Fathers Prayer", the Christian prayer that gives thanks to God. I believe this to be a great reality of our existence as humans. This idea of heaven is actually a place on earth, because heaven is a state of mind that you actually experience while you are here, and not an actual place to one day visit. Just like hell is not an actual place, but if you talk to enough people in life you will know that hell is also here on earth, and inside the heart and mind of any person who has seen darkness and turmoil in life. The majority of people understand what I am talking about but due to the nature of certain religious beliefs, someone might not fully choose to accept this understanding, and still live in fear of hell and in hope of heaven. It's the idea that these are actual places that we go once we die, and to live and dedicate their existence in life based on these. As I said before to each man go his own journey. What you choose to believe in life is exactly what will happen for you when you pass into the next period of existence. If you believe there is nothing after death, then that is your belief, and who am I or any other man to say otherwise. Nobody has that kind of wisdom or power over another human. So your beliefs will determine your life here and after.

Ok back to authenticity and living true to your calling and to yourself. Aligning yourself with this energy within you that connects you to all living things is still the principal thing. I find great inspiration by listening to someone else's interpretation of life, someone that is not quoting scripture or reciting an old hymn, but is speaking from their heart and their experience. This energy has the power to save lives and raise someone from death to life. Just like Jesus was resurrected we too have the power to save a person from death. And this is not something that should be taken lightly. If you can see the greatness that you are and the opportunity you have to save lives, then you would adhere to your calling at once and begin your journey towards becoming your true self by serving others. The gifts you will receive by doing so cannot be explained or imagined, only felt. I encourage you to feel this.

You are special and you have things to offer that no other human being has. This great truth has enough weight to remove every barrier that you have from not accepting yourself and connecting with the rest of humanity, if you just open your heart and mind. Live your life open to the possibilities and opportunity to share love and to serve another living thing. By doing so you are tapping into the very beginning of everything that ever was. You are actually becoming one with the circle of life and living your hearts song that only you have. The musical notes that come from within you will not fit onto anyone else's sheet music. Your symphony is your own, and you are the cello player and the trumpet player. It's all your creation, and the composition never ends. You will continually add notes to this great masterpiece and it will always sound magical because it comes from your deepest self and there is no other person on earth than create the music that you can. What will it sound like?

Chapter 7

Energy and stuff

You don't have to figure anything out, except who you really are. Why do you think I speak so much about authenticity in this book? Because when you go through life you will have your ups and downs and hang ups galore, but if you can simply understand that you have the power to shape and form everything that comes into your life, you would breathe a sigh of relief. The relief should come in the connection that you find within, and knowing that by coming from that place of wholeness you will invite more energy and situations into your life that honor that place. You get to decide what emotions you will feel and what thoughts you will hold in your mind, nobody else. Do you understand the weight to this statement? You are your own boss and you can have whatever in life you please!

Remember when I said everything is energy? Did I already say that? Well, if I didn't then I'm saying it now. EVERYTHING IS ENERGY. I want you to listen very closely right now... Everything outside of you responds to everything inside of you. What I mean by this is that your thoughts and your emotions are being sent out into the great dimension of energy that we live in. This 3rd dimension where we currently live is only one of the dimensions, but a higher dimension is where the energy from your thoughts and emotions go. Think of negative energy as the color red, in the form of a king size bed sheet flowing on a clothesline in the middle of a green meadow. You got that? You see the big red bed sheet blowing on a clothes line? Great! Now I want you to picture positive energy as a big white sheet next to the red one blowing in unison with the short bursts of wind that flow through the meadow. There you have it, positive and negative energy. Hold that image inside your mind.

  Ok now imagine that every time you think, or hold a thought in your mind that makes you feel bad, that a big red bed sheet gets released into the air, and every time you think or hold a thought in your mind that makes you feel good that a big white bed sheet is released into the air. These big sheets of energy go out into a higher dimension and you can only attract back to your life the same color sheets. So imagine that you had a negative thought and then you release this negative thought in the form of a big red sheet, and it leaves from inside your soul and goes out into another realm. The way energy works is that it only attracts back to it the same energy. So let's pretend the first negative thought was the thought that you will never be good enough to get the job that you want. The thought goes out and the process of attraction begins. Time cannot tell when your negative energy will be attracted back into your life, but just know that it's coming. The next day you go to get into your car and all of a sudden the big red sheet comes flowing back into your life, and you can't literally see this happening but for the sake of this lesson I want you to visualize and big red sheet flowing down and rushing towards you. The very same moment that the sheet reaches your body, you step into a large piece of gum on the pavement right before you get into your car. Alas the exchange has been complete! So because of your initial thought about you not being good enough to get the job you want, you have attracted into your life the situation where you have stepped into gum and now you have gum all over your shoe. Because energy just works this way. Whatever you think, or feel more importantly, goes out from you, and you can only attract the same exact energy from the previous or current feeling. You are a magnet, always attracting. This process is a universal law that connects all human beings, no matter what religion or belief system you have.

So you see how powerful it is to be in a place of feeling good? Being authentic and happy is the best way that you can live your life and attract more situations that keep you feeling authentic and happy. Unless of course you do not want to feel happy and in that case you should just continue feeling unhappy. But you should know that you DO have a choice.

Let's assume most people seek happiness but they are not yet fully convinced about this whole going within principal or getting to know their more authentic self. We can see this as the separation that someone is subject to somewhere between childhood and becoming an adult. There is a massive conditioning that occurs once you become old enough to start understanding things like money and responsibility. The world will never teach you that meditation or channeling energy will bring you money, or teach you more about a deeper connection to God. Because of this stigma people will believe that the only way to earn money is through hard work and dedication. And of course hard work and dedication can earn you money, sometimes lots of it, but the underlying truth is that allowing money to flow into your life is also a form of attracting and magnetism. Remember that when you have thoughts of doubt or anger you attract more events to make you doubtful or angry. The same is true about money. If you hold thoughts inside your mind about always having enough money and being so wealthy that you never have to worry about money again, then you will put into motion the law of attraction, and the universe will deliver to you more events and circumstances that allow you to have more money. It's absolutely true and it works one hundred percent of the time. Money is a mindset. Allowing the universe to fill your bank account up depends on your thoughts and emotions, not your hard work or dedication to your job. Of course whatever you must do to convince your own mind that you are worth lots of money is on you. If you cannot stretch your mind to understand that money can flow into your life without hard work, then you will forever be a slave to that work and that amount of pay. But if you can open your awareness to truth and energy, you can begin to allow money to flow into your life in abundance through forms that you could never fathom or understand on your own. Let money come in. You are more than deserving of being very wealthy and you can also use your money to serve this planet. So understand that as money starts to flood into your life you must treat it as a gift and give some of that gift to others also. If you start to feel greed or power because of money at any time in your life you need to very quickly reassess the situation and get back to an attitude of gratitude and service. No other energy can quickly reverse the flow of money into your life like greed can. Remember to think about the whole picture, the whole planet, and all livings things. You are here to be in service to them and the universe will not allow abundance in someone's life who does not give that abundance to others also.

      Can we just pause for a moment and breathe in some of the wisdom that has come into your heart and mind…

So you're just a great big mass of energy. And we know from science that billions of years have passed since the beginning of time and life on planet earth. Earth was literally formed from asteroids and space debris crashing into each other until our mass that we call home began to develop. This is sometimes what's known as the big bang theory. This is a very scientific theory and many people believe that this is how our planet began, but still many also believe that God created everything by speaking it into existence. These are both accurate to the one who believes them. Personally I believe in the more scientific approach to our existence but it doesn't make me wrong or right, it just makes more sense to me than anything else. So this is my truth and I express it without any regard to other beliefs or theories, just as you should express your truth whole heartedly. Knowing what I know about our universe and the galaxy I can speak about life on earth by using a truth that cannot be argued against, and that is the truth that stars and space matter are what first began to form life on our planet. The very basic elements like helium, carbon, oxygen, and hydrogen are the very first things that we can give credit to as starting the process of life here on earth. This is just science and many times science is truth, because it can be proven. So what this all means is that we as humans are made up of these elements also, and yes this can be proven. In essence you can understand this great truth of life that we were formed out of the stardust and space matter. Sink into that for a moment and remember this next time you look into the sky and feel the power of the light from the moon and the sparkle of the stars.

You may be thinking I jump around a lot with the topics that are being discussed and you're absolutely right. Creative thought and inspiration does not have a road map or a certain path that must be taken. The idea is to develop your awareness to this great gift that we have to tap into our highest potential at any given time, and receive inspiration and creative thought from the storehouse of infinite intelligence. This place can be understood like this… Have you ever had a time when you just got a wonderful idea that you were able to implement and it really helped you out? Well, this was a thought that was directly received from this place of higher wisdom. As I said, this place can be tapped into at any given time and the best way to invite new ideas into your mind is by remaining in a place of peace and happiness. Being in this state is allowing the energy to enter into your life, because remember that everything is energy, and your emotion is sending out the energy that you are giving off, and it can only attract back to you the same energy. So, as you are in a place of peace and happiness maybe you are waiting for an answer to your love life or your next career move. Because you are in this place of peace and happiness the universe wants to honor that and give you more of the energy of peace and happiness, meaning that anything you need answers to will be given to you, and all you have to do is be patient and wait. The answers will come as they always do. That's why you want to become as authentic as you can, and feel yourself deeply, because by doing so you're allowing all the answers to all the questions you have ever had to flow directly into your subconscious, and life becomes a beautiful waiting game. Are you patiently waiting for life to unfold for you, or are you chasing relentlessly for your answers? Life doesn't have to be hard. In fact the truth of life is the complete opposite. Life is natural, and life is abundant. YOU are this abundance.

Chapter 8

Relating to others

I am now ready to talk about relationships, and everything that has already been discussed can be applied to this topic. Energy, authenticity and attraction are your greatest tools when it comes to relating to people. Did you ever meet someone new and you did not have a good feeling about them from the first moment you shook their hand. In other words you got bad vibes from them? I think most of us have had this happen at least once or twice. That was you actually feeling that person's energy and sensing something negative about them, and most of the time we turn out to be right.

This goes back to our internal guidance system which I spoke about previously. Inside of us lives our intuition, and our intuition knows far better than our mind ever will, and by living from a place of trusting that inner guidance we can then have more healthy relationships in life and feel out situations and people, and see which ones would be good for us or not. Relating with others is also a very responsible thing to own because our energy affects everyone around us also. Owning your own feelings and energy will allow you to better relate to others. If you are wearing a mask and not really expressing how you are feeling people are going to sense that and it will affect the way they communicate and respond to everything you do. You might have heard the saying that being authentic and honest with yourself gives other people the courage and strength to do the same, and it's true. Remember, back to energy, everything you give off is drawing more of the identical back to you. If you are living with a smile when inside you are hurting then you are not showing other people your pain and your honesty. If you are not sharing your true self with others you are creating more situations and space for inauthentic people to come into your life that complement the energy that you have. And I don't know about you but I like to be around honest people. Your own energy will attract more people into your life who compliment that energy. The old saying misery loves company could not be truer when speaking about relating to others. If you are someone who complains all the time and live in a constant negative mindset you will not attract positive people into your life because they do not compliment your energy and you can only attract more negative people into your life. And the cycle can be hard to address for some people, because if they have a bunch of folks in their lives that speak and feel like they do why would they want to change? What's their motive? They feel like they have found their clique and until they look within themselves and desire a change they will likely continue with the same people. That's why when people are looking to change themselves for the better they have to immediately change the people they associate with. This is the quickest way to accomplish any kind of mindset change, surround yourself with the kind of people you want to be like. The laws of nature and energy are real and when you start understanding these laws you can start having the best relationships with the most amazing people you've ever met, because the universe will deliver the exact people you need into your life at the exact moment.

I've been trying to tell you that life is effortless, and it's a powerful truth that I'm confident you'll tap into when you're ready. When you are flowing with the natural process of your journey everything is given to you the exact moment you need it. It's a beautiful thing to understand and even more amazing to actually live in.

The golden rule says treat people the way you want to be treated. This is an exchange of positive or negative forces that will guide your actions and the way people act against you. If you are someone who belittles people or always sees the negative in someone then the universal law of attraction will cause people to look at you the same. There is such great balance on this planet, and the forces that hold everything together are the same forces that our emotions, thoughts and feelings become intertwined with, to create everything that flows into or out of our lives. There are great ancient people who have known this great wisdom, like Thoth the Atlantean or Pythagoras the Greek philosopher.

For year and years this great wisdom has been passed down from culture to culture and people to people. Being that the year is 2017 much of this wisdom has been lost and forgotten about. It does not make it any less powerful or life changing when understood and applied. People are starting to uncover these great truths and begin once again sharing them with others. The awareness of our collective consciousness is rising, and we are once again becoming beings that are highly in tune with ourselves and our lives. It is a process that each individual has to undergo separately but as a whole we are beginning to return to the great wisdom that was once a regular part of our culture and understanding as humanity.

Many times in life one will face adversity and overwhelming pain or sadness which will lead to suffering on a very personal and deep level. There is a powerful truth that I want to share with you about suffering, and this is also ancient wisdom that is practiced mostly by Buddhist peoples and Eastern cultures. Suffering is completely a choice. We are fully in control of what emotions we let come into our lives, and what thoughts and feelings we choose to focus on. Even in the worst of situations we can choose to respond in a completely different way which does not lead to suffering. Suffering is a great teacher and a powerful tool that allows us to change. A person will experience pain and anguish in life and either let it take them down into a dark and negative place, or to reach out for guidance and help. Answers can be found to all problems within one's soul, but what if the person hurting doesn't understand this. The path to fulfillment and peace is a personal path and no other human can walk your path for you. When you experience pain and suffering in life the best thing to do is to understand why you're feeling this way. So again, going back to authenticity and being true to one's self, you can more clearly understand your feelings and address what needs to be addressed so that you can get past your suffering and find your answers. The universe will place wise people into your life when you need them because we cannot do life alone. Teaching and wisdom must be passed down from those who are called to share, and instruct others on their journey through life.

     Give unto others as you would have them give unto you. Be a giving person. Live life fully and openly with other human beings. Share your heart and your mind with all those who need guidance. If there is something that a fellow person is going through or struggling with then it is your responsibility to instruct and guide them in the energy of love and service. This is also great wisdom that has been passed down through generations. If you choose to live life without any regard for other people then there is something inside of you that is not whole and has not found your answers yet. Only lost souls don't recognize they're worth and purpose. This is the reason for many of us who live our lives in service to others. We are here to help others find that place within them so in turn they can be of service to others, and collectively we can all share love and turn this planet into something beautiful and self-sustaining.

So the way you treat other people is probably the best way that somebody can determine whether you are a good person or not. For me personally it says everything I need to know about someone. Whether it be humans or animals that are being treated unfairly, the one acting out is immediately put into the file cabinet in my mind labeled "not for me". This means that I will not share my energy or space with that person. WE are personally responsible for who we let come into our lives or not, and to remove ourselves from situations with people who we do not want to be around, or get a bad feeling about.
Nobody else can understand what you personally feel inside, and you have to honor that place all the time, because ultimately you are the only one who knows exactly what you are feeling and what you need in each moment. In life I have found many people are too scared of what others will think to actually honor their own true feelings. Whether it's coworkers going out after work, or hanging out with the neighborhood

dads on Father's day, if there is something inside of you that does not feel good about it, and has nothing to do with your own personal social anxiety, then you should honor your intuition and do what you feel, no matter what anyone thinks. It is much better to stand alone and be happy than to be in a room full of people and feel miserable. You have the power of choice and you should use that power always.

Social anxiety is a form of not knowing your true self. Again, relating back to why authenticity is so important. It is a reliever of many types of stresses or discomfort. How much more could you bring to each situation you found yourself in if you were more comfortable in your own skin? The powerful and amazing influence you have on others is priceless, when you are living from a place of peace and confidence knowing that you are personally in control of your emotions and your thoughts, the energy that you give off is one that can save men and women from death. Yes, you have this power, and you should start understanding it so you can become a conduit of love to others.

Love is the ultimate truth of YOU. You are love. You are energy. You are the rose blooming. You are the grass that blows gently in the wind. You are the bird that soars high about the mountain. All of this represents the energy that you came from, and the energy that you will get back to. This is your journey in life. You may not know it yet, but by returning back to the source from which you came and everything that you are, you begin to fulfil your purpose and life becomes so much better than you could ever imagine it to be. This is why I guide others. This is why I instruct human beings to know themselves and to go within for their answers. This truth has the power to make you the greatest person who ever lived on this earth. But it's all your personal decision whether you meet this person, or continue following societal conditioning and live a life that is less than your absolute best. I want to inspire others to recognize this. To understand that there is more to life than we have been taught. There is much more to being happy than people understand. And there is much more to a life than the physical body. I'm here to teach energy and spiritual principles so that others can find a deeper understanding, and develop their own authenticity that will raise them to new heights that could not be attained had it not been for the stretching of their beliefs, and awareness of wisdom and truth.

We are here in this time together; nobody is separate from this great truth. Serve love and love will serve you. Love is the greatest goal in life.

Chapter 9

True wisdom

The further I get into this book the more I realize that I know very little. But it's certainly enough to offer into the great space of inspirational literature. Honestly, there may be very little you will find valuable about this book, but I'm completely confident that the majority of readers will find at least one thing that speaks to them, and I would encourage you to take that with you when you put this book down. Books are such an important part to your personal success and I can say that without a doubt in my mind. Without books I would not be who I am, and where I am today. There is no other way to quickly increase your intelligence and understanding than through reading. I am 33 years old, and I haven't always been like this. In fact I literally just started reading books regularly only 1 year ago. Within that year I have improved my mindset so much that I have found answers to lots of the questions I had about life. I was so inspired by my journey with reading books that I decided to write my own. The mental and spiritual impact that books had on my life is the same energy I hope to extend through my writing. It's my blessing that you find what you need when you need it.

The entertaining part of writing this book is that I have no idea what I'm doing. And by doing this I can prove some of the topics that I have already discussed, because I know this is going to somehow work out, I don't know how, but remember we don't have to know HOW things are going to happen, only WHY they are going to happen. My passion and desire to write a book is something that I have wanted to do for a while, and by following my heart and actually doing exactly what it wants it gives the universe and the laws that govern it the opportunity to work with me and provide everything I need on my journey. I have no idea how to publish a book. I have no idea how to market my book. I don't know what my book title is yet, or what the cover is going to look like. And that is really awesome to me. When you understand that things are always working out for your best interest than you never have to worry about how things are going to happen, only that they WILL happen!

There are also things inside your own heart that you have yet to honor and follow. Part of the reason to read books is to help yourself get to a place where you are more tapped into your heart and less tapped into you mind. Your thoughts are one of the most important factors in your own success, and keeping a positive mind will always deliver a positive life. But the opposite is that if you are negative inside your mind you will not be given a positive life. The mind is the forefront of control in your life. Without your belief in things, the things do not exist. I want to take this time to let you know that it's of utmost importance to think good thoughts about yourself. The only way I am completely sure of the power that this has is because there were many times in my life that I did not think good thoughts about myself. I have spent many years of my life lost and without direction which in turn made me feel all the feelings that come with having no purpose or vision for my life. It's a very dark place to be and I am very thankful that I got to experience those dark times because I would not completely understand how to get out of that season if I had never found myself there in the first place. Looking back now I can see how my experience can help others, and that's a huge motivation for me, to share my wisdom and experience with others. When we climb out of the dark I believe we become personally responsible to help others climb out of their darkness. I feel like it is just something engrained within us that connect us to that greater place where all knowledge and wisdom flows from.

    As we become part of that loving energy that desires to be of service we are tapping into our most authentic selves and becoming part of the natural flow of life that sustains itself and continues evolving into something beautiful. This is known as the great circle of life. If we love others and want the best for them we can be assured that the universe will respond to our heart and give us everything we need to be happy. Remember everything is energy, and love is the greatest. There is literally no greater way to guarantee your success than by loving yourself first, and loving others next. This is great wisdom that has been known for ages.

Can you look back at history and see how far we fell from this energy of love? Human beings have been evolving for a very long time and the fall of consciousness has greatly impacted our planet and formed it into its current state. Years and years of wars and turmoil and disharmony have all but wiped our civilizations out. Human beings are now destroying the planets resources at the most incredible rate, but despite this massive destruction our collective consciousness is evolving at a greater rate than ever. In fact just by reading this book you are becoming part of the hope of our existence. Isn't that cool?! Yes, you are making a stand and saying that you would like a better place to live and by taking responsibility for your own personal understanding you are evolving into someone that can stand up for what is right and make a huge difference in this world.

By giving back to the planet you are creating space for greatness in your life. You have superb opportunity to leave a legacy of service and love. Some of us are called to greater efforts than others and there is nothing wrong with being a small player in a huge game. Each individual person has talents and abilities that are unlike any other human, and I believe that once we identify these things we can begin to melt into the natural flow of existence and as long as we are being completely honest and coming from a place of love than everything will be added unto our lives without struggle. This includes everything from the material things like money and cars to the spiritual things like peace of mind and contentment. Once you are part of the natural flow of your life doing the exact things you want to do then life becomes unbelievably effortless, and you will only understand what I'm saying when you actually experience it. Society has told us to work hard for our money and our conditioning has made us think that if anything is worth having then it's worth struggling for, and these things are slowly being disproved as some of this higher wisdom is beginning to seep into our society and culture.

    Just know that YOU ARE LOVE. Your very essence is this eternal everlasting energy. You are the one who feels deeply and taps into your heart and soul at any given time and can access the power that gives life to all things. You just may not realize this yet. But the more you hold this vision of yourself the more you will become that person. Visualizing is one of the fastest ways to change anything in your life. When it is combined deliberate intention and honest emotion you can actually create anything and everything you want in your life. Have you ever seen the documentary called "The Secret"? I would highly suggest watching it, but the fact that you are reading such literature as this means that you are someone who is seeking truth, and you have quite possibly already seen it. I honestly believe when we are ready to advance our awareness or consciousness then the events that will do so are drawn into our life naturally. Remember everything is energy. If you are giving off the energy that wants to learn then naturally you will be given more situations and opportunities that you can learn from because that's just how energy works. Knowing this and applying it will absolutely blow your mind, so get ready for it.

I can't stress how important it is for you to always stay in a place of feeling good. You should literally make it one of the main things you hold inside your mind all the time. Always ask yourself, will this situation make me feel good or bad, and if the answer is bad then avoid it at all costs. It will literally catapult you to the next level of awareness in life because when you start to see things happen around you supernaturally and you realize that they are happening because you are in such a good place then you can begin to add your own personal touch to the fabric that is crafting your life. You are literally pulling everything into your life by willing it so through deliberate intention and belief. These are just laws of our universe and once you become accustomed to knowing that your thoughts and emotions affect everything in your life you will start watching how you think and feel. Everything you surround yourself with including music, people, and situations will have an effect on your thoughts and your emotions, and nobody else is responsible for what you let into your life except you. You see how you are the great creator of your existence? Can you start to understand now how you ultimately have the power to be who you want to be, and go where you want to go? There are absolutely limitless possibilities to what you can achieve and do in life. Once you start living authentic and tap into your most true self you will see doors open for you that support your journey and light your path to true fulfilment and purpose in this life.

      Sometimes you will have to leave things behind. People or habits or addictions might all be things that you must part ways with if you are to continue your journey towards truth and freedom. You must come to a place of commitment to your best journey. Your best self must be the one who steps forward and desires to be known. Above all else you must make this your goal and completely have no apologies for anything that must be changed for the betterment of this journey. You do not owe anyone any apologies. Some friends you'll never talk to again. Some music you'll never listen to again. You make your supreme goal feeling good and let nothing stop you from finding things in life that support that good feeling inside you. This is your highest goal and purpose in life.

When you encounter people who are truly and genuinely happy how does it make you feel? I can tell you a lot about your situation by the way you react to happy people. If you feel happy for that person and have desire to be around them then you are likely also a happy person. If that person makes you feel anxiety or uncomfortable then it's because you yourself are not truly happy. Going back to energy remember like can only attract like. So naturally unhappy people feel very apprehensive around happy people and happy people feel very uncomfortable around unhappy people. This isn't magic, it's just truth, and I promise you the more you can learn about this truth and many more truths of our existence the more aware of what is actually real you will become. You will start to place high value on these things and possibly be called to share what you have found with others, like I am doing with this book. I would love to encourage you to write a book, and if you need any guidance on this just talk to me and I'll tell you about my experience!

Chapter 10

Hiatus

Well I am coming back from a little time between writing due to some personal things I have been working through, so I can offer my experiences here in this next chapter about what I've learned. It seem wise to say that everyone is always dealing with something that we know nothing about, and we should always keep this in mind when relating to others. What I have been experiencing lately is something I have dealt with for a while and I'm now starting to move into a different space to completely remove these defects and behavior from my life.

It's my understanding that each person is born with predisposed conditions that make us more receptive to addictions or struggles in life. All of this is based on the physical and mental state of the parents at the time of conception, and what kind of energy transferred into the forming of the child. While we develop into adults many of us will develop the same anxiety and addictions that our parents themselves also struggled with. It's just genetics and science, and each person will walk their own journey towards understanding who they are, and what their struggles are. Our struggles do not define us but rather strengthen us to be of service to others.

When I think about all the identities that I've owned throughout my life I think back to all the times my ego would play huge roles in what I believed about myself. I would attach to these identities at any given time and really developed a comfort zone based on these limitations, when really that's all they were, limits to myself and my growth. In reality we have no limitations; we have just been conditioned to believe we do. Everyone wants to belong and be part of the bigger picture but very few of us will actually take a stand and break out of the norm to discover a whole new level of existing. But once we do we can free ourselves from our old self, and being a whole new journey with no limiting beliefs about who we are, and we can just hold space in the moment and live from our hearts in everything we do. Having this experience will absolutely catapult you into situations and opportunities that you would have not had the chance to find otherwise.

Being present in each moment without speculation about what's to come is one of the most freeing things to feel. This divine state of being is something that can invite multitudes of creative and inspiring thoughts into your life, and allow energy to transform your heart and mind into your most authentic self. We all have so much potential inside of us and very few actually tap into it, but those who do are the ones who change the world and bring something unique to our existence that can influence millions of lives.

I am feeling a sense of anxiety with writing this book. I am not someone who can draw out stories and make things longer than they need to be. I tend to be directly to the point and when a logical concern is word count and trying to get to a certain quota, it can be a headache knowing how much material I've covered and how many words I still feel like I need to get. So this morning I started my day with some coffee on the balcony of my apartment as I sat with my cat Leo and gathered my thoughts for the day. I like to spend time every morning in reflection and visualizing the day ahead of me and what I want to accomplish. In the morning upon waking your brain is emitting what is called Alpha waves. When your brain is in Alpha it is actually the strongest frequency that is emitted to create and attract things into your life, so visualizing is really important during this time. After my coffee I turn some music on and get myself in the mood to work out. I walk into my bedroom and make my bed and say a little prayer standing in front of my prayer table as I turn my salt lamp off and put on some gym clothes and walk into the kitchen. After my workout I take a shower and leave for work.

This is my standard routine for the morning and I'm telling you this because having a routine to start your day is a very powerful way to start on a positive note and find an optimistic mindset to guide you through your day. We know that being in the correct mindset will allow you to feel good, which will in turn attract more of that energy into your life and create a wonderful day. Owning your happiness and how you spend your morning is a big responsibility. Nobody can make you wake up in a grateful mood and start your day with a smile. This is a conscious decision on your part and I encourage it daily.

    At any given time in your life you will be working on something. This is almost a guarantee. Unless of course there are conditions present in your life that allow you to remain stagnant and still survive and live happy. I am not someone who can live happy by remaining stagnant, and I don't think you are either. So we are in a constant process of working through things in our lives, whether at our job or in our personal lives. And this is a good thing. This is something that will ensure great success in your life. How many of us take on too many things at one time and end up getting none of them done? We get so overwhelmed because we cannot dedicate the time we need to each individual thing but rather try to juggle a few big things at one time. I am actually working on getting better at this. My mind is always processing information due to my hyperactive nature. So in essence it's very difficult for me to focus on just one thing for a very long time, I get increasingly bored very rapidly. It really is quite a learning process to get to know yourself and learn how to best do things in life to be the most benefit to your journey. I personally know that I must have more than one thing in my life that excites me, like a hobby or something active. I like living life like this, and I respect that about myself and do not struggle to change it, but rather get into the flow of who I am and use it as my strength, because this is one of the qualities that set me apart from others, and that is awesome. Just like you have things that set you apart, you should encourage and grow those things with pride. So this keeps life exciting, the fact that you can either be always working on something outside of you or something inside of you, which ensures us that we can never grow stagnant. Your body begins to die when you refuse to learn or have an attitude of unwillingness to progress in your journey. It has to. Every cell in your body responds to every thought in your mind. If your mind thinks "I'm done here", then your body will say "Ok", and begin deteriorating rapidly. You will invite sickness and disease and before you know it you will be on your last days here.

So what are you currently learning about yourself? What are you currently working towards in your life? Me personally I am actually preparing myself for massive success in my finances and my relationships. I wake up every day knowing that my financial freedom is right around the corner and I patiently expect to make very large amounts of money in the near future. I also anticipate the feeling I will have when I meet the special girl that I will fall in love with and how amazing that will be. These are the two most important things I am working towards right now in life. And honestly the work does not feel like work at all, it feels like life. Because this is the life I want to manifest. This is the life I want to attract into my existence, and I will. Remember the power of the mind and energy, and holding the thoughts that you want to appear in your life. It's all mental. This doesn't mean it is easy by any means, because there are mental road blocks that I must fight daily if I want to attract this life for myself. For instance, there are thoughts from my old mindset that sometimes pop into my head and tell me that I'm not good enough or that I am not going anywhere, and knowing that these are silly ways the brain tries to distract me from my purpose is my greatest asset. The ability to detach from your thoughts will be one of the most beneficial things you can do. Our thoughts are constantly coming and there is literally no way to stop them, unless you undergo some rigorous meditation which I highly suggest on occasion. We don't have the power to stop our thoughts throughout the day but we do have the power to choose which ones we let effect our emotions. Often times I am reminded of thoughts of my past and memories of things that I enjoyed, and sometimes memories of things that I did not enjoy so much. At that moment it is up to me to decide which memories I choose to dwell on, if any at all. It is said many times to not think about the past because it is the past, and I agree. I try to remain as much in the present as I can but this also is something that I constantly work on because the brain will do what it does and keep thinking of all kinds of stuff throughout the day, so it's a real chore to remain present in each moment. A big source of unhappiness is dwelling in the past or worrying about the future. Stay present, my friends.

    Well I had a good workout this morning, so before work at Wal-Mart I thought that I would have corndogs for breakfast. So in preparation for my yummy stick food I will talk briefly about nutrition. You must not stress too much over the things that you eat, but let the ultimate dictator to your diet be the way you look in the mirror naked. Yes, I'm telling you to judge yourself, judge your body. Yes. This is not a crazy thing to do it's actually quite smart if you ask me. Look at yourself naked in the mirror every day and if you start not liking what you see, or you start gaining a little extra around your waist then change your diet and start exercising more. The other way to monitor your nutrition is to know how your body feels internally. This is something that you just have to tune into and become aware of. Obviously if you eat a whole cheese pizza by yourself and your body feels heavy and all you do is lay on the couch then it's probably not a good thing to do. All I am saying is that each person is individually responsible for his/her own body or health. When people can take full responsibility for this they can have the body and health that they want, and encourage others to be healthy also.

Time for corndogs.

Chapter 11

Visualization

If you learn nothing else this could be the most important thing to consider. I'm placing lots of energy and empathy on this subject because it holds some serious weight, and I'm sure you've learned a bit about this in your own life, or at least heard of it before. Doesn't matter if you understand it yet or not, I'm going to explain this in the best way I can.

YOU MUST HOLD IT IN YOUR MIND IF YOU WANT TO SEE IT IN YOUR LIFE.

I could literally stop the chapter right there and just tell you to go close your eyes and repeat what I just said one hundred times, and you're welcome to do that if it helps you understand how serious this is. Go ahead, I'll wait.

Great people of higher wisdom have always known this and have dedicated their life to teaching others. Emerson, Einstein, Edison, Carnegie, Lincoln, MLK, etc.… Seriously, this is something that if understood and applied can give you literally anything you want in life. I'm teaching you this because I'm living it, and I want you to live it also. We all deserve to know this great wisdom, but they don't teach you this stuff in school do they? No, because they want to keep you in the dark, so you can be of better service to those who control everything.

Let me give you an example so you can see how this works. In order for you to change anything about yourself you must be convinced that you are worthy of it. So if you want to stop being such an angry person you have to agree that you deserve to be a happy person. If you cannot first come to this agreement than don't even try to change, because it just won't happen. Our belief is the strongest power we have in our lives. So we must first believe that we deserve the change we are seeking, and then we must only hold inside our minds that new person that we want to become. This is what is called visualizing. You must begin to think of yourself in situations before that used to make you angry, and visualize yourself remaining calm and collected. This image you must hold inside your mind constantly throughout the day, and anytime you are not sleeping, and then before you fall sleep also. So in essence you are creating the person you want to become by holding the thoughts in your mind of exactly what that person looks like. Do you see how wonderful this is, or is it just me? You can literally change anything and become anyone you want to become, the power lies within you.

Now that you understand what visualization is let's move on. It's not only important to hold images in your mind of what and who you want to become, but to also feel the feelings of what it will feel like to be that person. This is where the real magic happens. Remember that everything is energy and every time you feel an emotion you are sending out energy into the universe that can only draw the same energy back to it. So if you feel what it will feel like to be a calmer and collected person the universe will respond and give you more situations to feel calm and collected about, therefore once again you are the ultimate creator of your life. People that know this great wisdom are magical people. They walk with purpose and they know how to get anything they want in life. Sometimes the things you want come quickly and sometimes they come slowly, it only depends on your level of commitment to the thoughts that you hold in your mind, and the emotions you feel in your body.

    The corndogs are good by the way.

    Tuning into yourself and living authentic and honest can only intensify all of this great wisdom I am sharing with you. But if you are not tuned into yourself and not living life honestly you will unfortunately have no power to use any of this. Remember we live in a planet that is governed by universal laws of nature and energy, and if we are not living in our most natural state we can live than we have no opportunity to become part of this magical flow of abundance that is available to us. Going with the flow of life and nature is the most wonderful thing that we can experience as humans, but we must conquer ourselves first. We must work through our hardships and struggles to discover and accept our true selves and begin to unwind all the false things that we thought we knew or thought previously. This is the journey to enlightenment and awareness. The wool has been pulled over the eyes of millions of people and it's each person's individual responsibility to know this, and to discover truth and seek what is real. Once you begin to come out of the darkness of societal conditioning and mental control life really will begin to open up, and great things are ahead to all of those who seek to know the truth.

    One of my favorite quotes that I live my life by is this. "Man know thyself, and thou shalt know the universe, and God". This is a quote by Pythagoras. When I first heard this I didn't quite understand it, but as I progressed forward in my journey it all started to make sense. There is no separation between the universe, God or us. WE are all part of this great wisdom. WE are one. WE are connected. So by getting to know myself, I was getting to know God, and the universe. This wisdom blew my mind when I finally started understanding it and I threw myself even farther into self-inquiry and awareness. Knowing that there is no separation between the universe, God and myself really launched me into a deep understanding that very quickly made me move away from any single religious belief that I had previously in life through my experience with Christianity. I knew that religion was such surface level stuff that wasn't for me anymore, although I always respect religion and religious people, I just began seeing it in a different light. This idea that I was one with everything was a beautiful thing and I attained a level of peace and freedom that I never found in church. This is what I would call a huge milestone in awareness and understanding. When you learn something that allows you to completely peel off your old clothes and old ideas and step into something new and beautiful. I absolutely love this kind of thing and I want people to experience this just as I have. Maybe not literally the same way, but to have such an awesome shift that it completely changes you for the better and helps you move forward in greater truth and freedom. Because it really does make you feel free. This should be a huge motivation to learn and understand as much as you can about yourself and about life. To hit these milestones and to experience this freedom is something I encourage people to strive for all the time.

      I don't know about you but I am someone who likes to always have something to look forward to. I like having a trip planned or an event coming up that I can anticipate every day when I wake up. It's just a cool feeling to have something to think about that excites you, and something you can focus on and work towards. Sometimes there is what I call dead time. This is when you have nothing to look forward to, or nothing that is currently making you feel excitement. But this can be perceived in a different way by thinking about what you're grateful for and always staying in gratitude. If you remain in a state of gratitude all the time you can always depend on that feeling and not need the feeling of excitement of what's to come. But for me, I am an adrenaline junkie and I sometimes struggle with this dead time because I really like to feel excitement. Ever since I was a little boy I loved things that excited me. Things that made me feel alive. And unfortunately sometimes the things that make you feel the most alive are the things that are illegal or are dangerous for you. And yes I have indulged in illegal activities throughout my life. For some reason I always feel more alive the closer I am to death or danger. I don't know if there is something wrong with me or what, but I don't think I'm the only one who feels this way. But some people think I'm absolutely crazy for thinking this way, and that's ok. Living life on the edge isn't so bad after all. It's really quite exciting! And as long as I am having fun and not hurting anyone, then I'm all in!

Whatever excites you, make your life be about that. It's so important to be involved with things that make your soul come alive, otherwise what is life for?! I am seriously encouraging you right now that if you are not doing things in your life that make you come alive with excitement than you need to change something. As human beings we need to feel fulfilment and excitement. Life is not meant to be boring and dull. This is a beautiful and amazing opportunity we have to be made manifest as human beings on this planet in this time, and we should make the absolute most of it by reaching deep into our souls and getting to know who we are, and doing the things that we want and like, because we can, and we should. There is nobody else exactly like us. If we do not express ourselves than I am afraid the world will be missing out on the experience it will have with us in the mix. Nothing would be the same without you. This world would be completely different if you were not here. So be here and be alive! Bring all your emotions and all your thoughts together to express the deepest nature of who you are and why you are here. And then inspire others to do the same!

What if we are running out of time? Who knows for sure how much more time we have here on this planet. An asteroid could hit tomorrow and totally wipe our existence out. If that is not enough motivation for you to get up and make your life something amazing then I just honestly don't know what else to tell you. Of course there are some people that don't care to be or do anything better in life. These are what I call unhappy people. And these people are not part of our tribe. The fact that you are reading this book tells me that you are my tribe. You are part of the humans that exist to enjoy life. You are part of the tribe that helps others and loves life. You are part of the great thinkers and great dreamers, and I'm happy to have you on my team. Thank you for being born!

Ending this chapter I just want to say how proud I am of you to have made it this far in the book. I'm not going to say this has been an easy task for me to write a book at all. But once I started writing the wisdom and knowledge just continued to come flowing from my fingertips and onto the computer screen so I just went with it. Although looking back at my first few chapters, they are pretty gnarly so I think I will probably have to go back and edit a lot in the beginning. But once I got used to the fact that I was only sharing my heart and mind with you it started to flow much more easily. And letting go of the outcome of what you would think about my book also helped me move forward and continue. This process is as much for me as it may be for you, and I may actually be getting way more out of this than you will. But thanks for being part of this journey anyway.

Chapter 12

Accepting responsibility

You have been blaming situations and people your whole life. Did you know that? I don't think anyone is exempt from this. We shy away from responsibility and try to deter the spotlight from ourselves many times throughout our lives. I am as guilty as the next person. There has been so many times in life where instead of admitting to something being my fault I point the finger and blame it on the weather, or the cat, or someone completely random. By engaging in this kind of fallacy we can only build up more of an inauthentic attitude about ourselves and distort our self-image to the point where we no longer know what is right or wrong. And this can be really scary. I'm sure you can remember particular times, maybe when you were younger, where you engaged in this type of delusion. Whether you were doing it to get out of trouble, or elude someone from knowing the truth about a certain situation. I think we have all been there. The dangerous part of doing this is that if you continue lying to yourself and others it will be much harder when you actually have the spotlight shine on you, and it's time for you to take responsibility with something important. You will be ill prepared if your whole life you have deterred the attention elsewhere.

I'm going to be in your face a little bit and say that everything that has happened to is YOUR fault. Now I'm being realistic here so don't twist this into something it's not. If you lost a parent or have a best friend that killed themselves, those things are not your fault. Don't be a baby and get offended, just listen. I know you're sensitive, but stay with me.

Your health is your fault. Your finances are your fault. You job is your fault. Your significant other is your fault. This can be regarded as a good thing, or a bad thing. I say the word fault but I really mean responsibility. You are completely in control of all of these things in your life, so you cannot blame them on anything or anyone else. You will find a serious amount of freedom when you realize and admit to this. Only by taking full responsibility for your life can you advance on to the next level of awareness and freedom, therefore being more authentic and honest in your being. If you want to change any one of these things guess what, you have to be the one to make the changes. If you are unhappy with your job or your finances or your spouse you cannot blame anyone else except yourself for being upset or unhappy with these things. You got yourself here, and if you really want change then you have to make the change. Why are we so scared to take responsibility? I can tell you why. Because nobody likes to admit that they are wrong. Rather than admit we are wrong, human beings will find every possible outcome that stretches the truth to prove that we are not guilty, and continue to live in the shit that we created in the first place. Humans can be very strange.

How aggravating is it when you personally know someone who is living a lie and not taking the responsibility for something? I absolutely cannot stand it. In fact, if there are people around me or in my life that show signs of this type of behavior I immediately remove myself from their lives. This kind of attitude is extremely toxic and can only infect all of the people who choose to remain part of it. If you are anything like me you may call people out immediately if you sense any kind of dishonesty or falsehood. Like I said, I won't allow myself to be part of this type of energy, and if somehow I find myself in a situation then it's my immediate responsibility to remain true to myself and call some bullshit if I see it, no matter if it hurts anyone or not. And yes you might consider this a bad habit because some people just aren't ready to look at the role they play, and would rather continue living their lie. But that's ok, staying true to myself is more important than impressing others, and I would encourage you to believe this too.

Skating around the truth is actually a normal part of our society. It was not always like this, but as we progressed through time and gradually soared forward through the 3rd dimension into the current time we find ourselves in, we have gotten increasingly worse about this topic. Why is that do you think? Why as a society have we gotten worse and not better? Well, I can muster up my best conclusion to this if you want to listen.

As human beings we have fallen from our ultimate reality, which is having a collective consciousness around unity and love. The things that have divided us include pride, ego and greed. What I mean is that our ultimate downfall has been due to the lack of connection that we have within ourselves as individuals, and our human race as a whole. The lack of understanding that we have about our own self has contributed tenfold to this extreme state that we find our planet in currently. The thought that we are all divided by things like religion, race and creed is the biggest lie that we have adapted over the millennia. These are differences between us but they do not divide our human race as a whole. WE are all connected with one another, and with love. This is our ultimate highest understanding, but is also something that not many people seek to understand in life. We are so focused on our circumstances and our money that we don't have a desire to pursue knowledge and wisdom about unity and love. Some people do a great job at pretending also, which goes back to the title of this chapter. People will pretend to be part of this higher wisdom and understanding by attending church and feeling a sense of connection with their congregation but failing to acknowledge the rest of the planet and all the teachings of all the people that inhabit our world. I would encourage you, don't ever use religion as a means of dividing the human race. I think it's absolutely absurd to separate ourselves because of our belief systems and upbringings. You can be part of your religion and accept other religions without the pride and ego that you are better than the other. Aristotle said it is the mark of an educated mind to entertain an idea without accepting it. I hope you can also learn to respect and honor another man's religion, even if it is not what you believe in, and if a house were burning down that you would not determine which person you saved first due to their belief in religion. Please educate yourself and just love yourself and others.

       There is power in understanding. Education and reading books are really an amazing thing, and I've mentioned it before already but I'm talking about it again because it deserves to be mentioned a hundred times over. Some of the wealthiest people in the world were also some of the most educated. Knowledge is the one thing that can bless your life beyond measure. We should constantly evolve our education and knowledge. There is no cap to how much we can learn in life. If I could encourage you to make it a top priority in life to learn as much as you can than you would open more books and seek wisdom from more sources. This is such a personal journey that it's nearly impossible for me to explain the benefit that this will have in your life. It cannot be explained, only experienced. I hope you'll commit to it.

 With your commitment I would also encourage you to start right now and begin a new commitment to being completely responsible for everything in your life. Take hold of absolutely everything, the good and the bad and the ugly. Own it and feel the connection deep within yourself that serves something bigger than you. The legacy that you will leave depends on you being committed to this great wisdom. For it is my assumption that you will have very little impression on those you come into contact with unless you are completely responsible for your life and your actions. Don't you want to leave a positive mark on people that you meet? Don't you want to leave this place better off than when you got here? I think you do. You would not be reading this book right now if there was not a greater calling on your life in which you are currently pursuing. Applying the things that you learn will be the ultimate manifestation of the improved awareness in your life. Living a more authentic life and living your truth and sharing that with others I believe is your ultimate destiny. I'm really glad to be part of your journey and I send you blessings and energy on your journey.

 So let's take a less serious turn and speak once again about corn dogs. I am having them for breakfast again today and I'm super excited. I had a great workout at the gym this morning and I need the proper and sustaining nutrition that corn dogs offer. My favorite thing to dip my corn dogs in is mayonnaise. It's actually my favorite condiment. Also mustard is a great delectable sauce for the dog of corn on stick. Whichever situation you find yourself in when approaching a meal, it is best to be prepared. I'm ready.

      I hope you drink lots of water every day. Do you? Water is so freaking important to your body that its literally the most valuable thing you can put into it, besides corn dogs. If you can practice drinking up to a gallon a day I can promise you that your health will improve. It doesn't matter what you're trying to do with your body, the more water you drink the faster you will accomplish your fitness goals. You can literally ask anyone in the health and fitness world and they will agree with me. I was a personal trainer for 10 years and I've held two national level certifications. So rather than have to go ask a health and fitness professional about drinking water and the importance of it, just listen to me. Drink more water!

      So the chapter started off with responsibility and is ending with corn dogs and water. I like that. But it's literally your responsibility if you want to eat corn dogs or drink water. You see how this works? Whether or not you begin to apply the fact that corn dogs are a super nutritious gift from the Gods, or that water is the elixir of life is all on you. You cannot blame anyone if you don't believe this stuff. And of course I'm being sarcastic about the corn dogs, they are probably the least nutritious thing you can put into your body. And I'll show you an example of how someone can evade responsibility here. Let's say someone starts eating corn dogs all day, every day. And instead of researching more into it they place the blame on me and say, "Well I read somewhere that corn dogs were the most nutritious thing you can put into your body", and completely evade the responsibility for it. Not saying that anyone would do that but I'm using it as an example. People can be so crazy and blame anything they can on their actions and outcomes in life instead of owning it and accepting their mistakes. I suggest you become aware of this behavior in others and do your best to avoid those people.

Chapter 13

Sharing is caring

There is a capability inside of you that still waits to be discovered. Did you know that? This is something I know about you, and I'm not psychic. I can nearly absolutely promise that around less than 10% of people are actually living to their undeniable full potential. And even those people are constantly growing and learning and becoming better, because these people know that there is limitless potential. There is no finish line! There is no final destination. You can absolutely do anything and be anyone you want to be. And when you get tired of being that person, you can become someone else, and continue on this never ending saga of life! If that doesn't excite you then you're just dead on the inside and you have yet to fully come alive to what is real. But the fact that you are reading this book is developing your mindset around this and I'm happy for your growth. If you feel really compelled to thank me, the best way you could do so would be to share this book with others. Because what I want is to teach people the great freedom that is found in the truth, so please tell your friends and family about this and encourage them to read it.

The neat part of the relationship that you have established with me now is that it feels so close doesn't it. Don't you feel like we have known each other for years already? You know why that is? It's because of my transparency, and ability to deliver my mind and spirit directly to these pages. What that does for you is connect you deeply to your own soul. The part of you that resonates with the words I speak and the things I discussed. There is a strong energy that you have felt already many times while reading this book. You know what that is? It's your spirit and my spirit becoming one. It's a massive shift in your own consciousness that fully accepts yourself, and is becoming more aware of your own truth. It should feel pretty awesome. You're welcome. And you have the same ability to have this identical effect on those around you. All it takes is complete acceptance of yourself, and a release of all negativity and fear. In this way you can become the most authentic version of who you are and have a very powerful influence on others. Do it.

A great idea is nothing without the faith that it will happen. It's completely void of any value if you do not believe in it. Our faith is a powerful thing that creates our lives. Belief makes everything real. You can only manifest that which you believe in. If you want to own a golden retriever, you have to visualize yourself playing with the dog and have the strongest emotions of joy and happiness surrounding this event. By doing so your energy will pull the very desire into your life and you can have your new puppy and life will be awesome. I've already spoken about this stuff earlier in the book and it's super important so remember it.

Did you know that your whole body is vibrating? If you broke yourself down to the most pure of particles and molecules you would see that you are constantly in motion. Your energy is reflected by your thoughts and emotion. So the amount of motion and vibration that is found in each molecule of your body is all based on your feelings and thoughts. That's why when you feel really good you almost feel like you're buzzing right? You can literally feel your body and sense that amazing energy that you are giving off. The same is true if you are in a bad mood. The energy of your body slows down so much that you go into a depression, and it's like all you want to do is be lazy or sleep, because your molecules are not vibrating very rapidly and your energy is very low. You can literally feel when people are in a good or bad mood from the vibes that they are giving off. This is real stuff I'm talking about, educate yourself about it! I can only scratch the surface for you but I hope to make you more interested about this so you can really find some great truth and learn how important it is to be positive and happy. Hatred is literally the lowest vibration that you can experience. And love is the greatest. Why do you think love is so powerful and so important? It is our ultimate reality and the greatest form that we can find ourselves surrounded in. And when we are in the energy of love, anything is possible, and we are inviting the best and most powerful opportunities into our life that will encourage our greatest growth and give us everything we want in life, period.

Learn how to love better and everything in your life will get better. Make love your absolute mindset all the time. Filter every action and every thought with love.

Open your hands right now, well read this first and then put the book down and open both of your hands up and look at them. I want you to realize how much freedom there is in not holding onto anything. This exercise is for you to understand that abundance and blessing will freely come into your life, and there is little you can do with your own strength to keep or hold onto them. You're not even supposed to because they so freely came into your life, so keeping your hands open and using this as a representation of how effortless it is to obtain everything you need is something I hope you can really wrap your mind around. All you literally have to do is be happy and be in love. I don't mean be in love with someone like in a relationship, but live in love. Live in the energy of love. Miracles will continue to manifest into your life if you can remain in love. I promise. I'm sure most of you have experienced this already so I'm just hammering home this great truth!

Waiting for more inspiring thoughts...

Or maybe I don't have to wait for anything special, but just keep typing and something will magically develop. Yea I think I'll do that. It's a little cloudy today and the sky looks pretty cool. Shades of blue paint the canvas with white clouds in the distance. Are you someone who is impressed by such things? There is so much beauty and magnitude around us at any given time but people can become so busy with life that they don't take the time to look at the sky and enjoy the wonder that is our planet. I love being aware of the sky and the sun and the moon and the stars. I love connecting to these things every day. By connecting to these things I am connecting to myself, because I am made of the particles of the universe, and the stars. And you are too! You are literally so amazing that I cannot explain it. Every human life is a miracle of love and creation. Hold people in high regard knowing that they are special in this way, and hold yourself there also. WE are all connected in a way that can never be explained, but only felt. I hope you currently feel this, or that one day you can begin to feel it.

Chapter 14

A special teacher

There is a special understanding that I want to share with you now in regards to the greatest teacher you will ever know. This teacher is poised and ready to show you all the secrets of your life and all the things needed to achieve what you want to achieve. Your access to this teacher is unlimited and I have spoken much about this inner guidance system that every human being has and its time you become more aware of why this is your greatest teacher you will ever know.

In essence you are the only one who can teach yourself anything. What I mean by this is that you can read a book or take education courses about subjects and things that you wish to desire learning about, but ultimately the knowledge has to be filtered through your own being. This guidance system inside can determine whether the information you are learning is valid information or not, as long as you are tuned into your inner self. This guidance should act as a filter to anything that enters your life, no matter what. This connection within is not something to be taken lightly and one cannot attain this divine connection without knowing that he or she is also divine. I spoke of this in earlier chapters, but it's basically the fact of knowing that there is no separation between you and God, or this Great Spirit energy. When you can really wrap your mind around this truth and start to live in your divine self all the time then you will know that you hold the answers to all your greatest questions in life. The point is to slow down long enough to develop this kind of awareness, and to continue growing the strength of your faith in which you feel this truth.

When you are living in your highest self, you are connected to all the divinity that has ever been known. You are one with the universe and there is a storehouse of infinite intelligence that becomes available to you whenever you need it. The process for attaining what you want is very easy. The first thing is that you have to have a deep yearning for whatever it is you want. You have to literally think and feel this emotion of knowing this thing, and by doing this you will begin to pull the wisdom into your life, and sometimes the answers will just come rushing down into your awareness and you will be given the answers instantly, or sometimes people will be added unto your life that will deliver these answers to you. However the answer is found you are the one who attracted it. It is your energy that created the pull for the attraction to occur. All your desires will be made into your reality as long as you understand this great universal law. It is constantly at work and you can find your answers to everything simply by having a desire to find them.

Some people will say that the law of attraction does not work or that the only way to get anything is to pray to God. Well the only thing I can tell you about that is that each person's belief will be the reality of their lives. I am someone who develops a belief in things much greater after I actually see the belief work in my life. These laws of the universe and understanding of the human mind, and the power of the heart, always work when I apply them correctly, and I believe they can for anyone.

I'm happy to have shared the things I shared with you in this book and I'm thankful for the inspiration I received and divine guidance that helped me write this.

I just want to take a moment and honor the energy that allowed me to write this book.

Forever, grateful.

CPSIA information can be obtained
at www.ICGtesting.com
Printed in the USA
LVOW10s0621021117
554734LV00025B/375/P